HOW TO FLY
AROUND THE WORLD
(ALMOST FOR FREE)
AS AN AIR COURIER

A COMPLETE REPORT ON HOW TO TRAVEL
VERY INEXPENSIVELY

BY: WILLIAM HALKEN

HOW TO FLY
AROUND THE WORLD
(ALMOST FOR FREE)
AS AN AIR COURIER

ISBN 1-882330-11-0

I would like to acknowledge:

Close family and friends who supported my enthusiasm for this project, especially my wonderful wife Jane. Also, special thanks is due to Lorraine W. for her expert editing skills.

William Halken

TABLE OF CONTENTS

SECTION ONE

SECTION TWO

DISCLAIMER

This book is intended for use only as a background tool, and is based upon the information and perceptions gathered by the author and verified by the publisher.

At the time of printing, the information contained herein was judged to be accurate.

The author and the publisher do not endorse any particular airline or air courier company.

SECTION ONE

P
A
R
T

1

HOW TO USE THIS BOOK

This book is arranged in five major sections, with each section comprising the elements necessary to fully understand and participate with the air courier process. In **Section One**, you are introduced to the foundations of the air courier program. In **Section Two**, you are shown how to begin and follow through with actually taking your flight. **Section Three** is a comprehensive index of the major courier company contacts. **Section Four** is a comprehensive index of major courier company contacts of non-U.S. gateway cities. **Section Five** is a summary with additional helpful information, and answers to some of the most frequently asked questions about air courier travel.

It is highly recommended that you take time to totally understand each section of this book before moving on to the next section. When you fully understand these sections as explained, there will be very little left to chance when you take your first courier flight. If you think of this book as the focus of your first steps into a whole new field of skill and adventure, you are sure to succeed in activating a new exciting avenue of travel in your life.

Happy Travels!!!

P
A
R
T

2

OVERVIEW

START WITH ENTHUSIASM!

Travel can transform your life! The tools in this book will show you how to see the world at an amazingly low price.

You are about to actualize incredible global travel on the wings of the modern world, in vessels not even dreamed of one hundred years ago! People once traveled for days and months under great risk and discomfort to cross a great landmass or ocean. You will travel at near supersonic speeds, miles above the earth, and the cost will be minimal.

Think about it! When you travel as an air courier, practically the entire world will be available to you. Begin your journey by going to the library, or your favorite bookstore. Gather up information about those far away places you've always hoped to see, but never knew if, when, or how you could.

As you begin reading about these far away dream places, make a list and prioritize those desired places you wish to visit. It is this list you will evaluate against the destinations of the courier companies you select for your journeys. As your research progresses, so should your enthusiasm for this new venture in your life. This is the first step you must attain before moving on in this book.

YOUR PRELIMINARY GROUNDWORK

The first step in becoming a competent air courier lies in forming the 'Big Picture' in your mind of what being an air courier truly is. To trace the basic concept of a courier back to the misty dawn of time, we would find that there were always two elements involved. The first was a special type of important cargo (often time sensitive), and the second was a specific individual accompanying this special cargo.

This special cargo can be further broken down into two types. The first type is cargo which would be of a valuable nature to everyone, such as cash. The second type would be valuable to a select few individuals, such as a business document. Therefore, the type of cargo basically dictates which type of individual accompanies it. Enthusiastic individuals such as ourselves are regularly used to accompany shipments of the 'business document' type of cargo, and the 'cash' cargo would be accompanied by a special organization such as 'Brinks'.

In both cases, either cargo is of a very important nature. The 'business document' requires speed; and the 'cash' requires special protection, and possibly speed. The purpose of this book is solely to inform you as to what it takes to be a "business document" type of courier.

The aspect of speed is attained by the simple fact that modern day international passengers claim their baggage immediately upon passing through customs upon arrival at their destination. The contrast of this is evident when you consider that

18

regularly shipped air cargo goes through approximately five processing steps upon arrival at its destination. With this regular air cargo, one could expect three to five days before a delivery is completed. On the other hand, the courier company utilizes your baggage allowance and speeds delivery of your accompanied goods to their international destination overnight, or very soon thereafter. How they actually do this while charging you so little will be discussed in depth later on in this book.

Next, to understand how the early courier evolved into the present day air courier, we need to take a close look at the times in which we live. The invention of the jet engine by two independent inventors, the first, Sir Frank Whittle, who wrote of "Future Developments in Aircraft Design" in his 1928 thesis, and Dr. Hans Von Ohain, in 1935 while a doctoral student of physics at the University of Gottingen in Germany, resulted in bringing the world to the edge of one of its most important breakthroughs.

Their great discovery culminated in a grand practical application in the late 1950's when the world was introduced to the wonders of commercial high speed jet transportation. Although this incredible achievement is now taken for granted, and even largely complained about, its importance has propelled the world into the modern times as we know them. In addition, it has made the opportunity for very high speed air courier travel possible.

The second step is done in parallel with the research you are undertaking in Section One, Part 2 ("Start with Enthusiasm"). This effort involves turning to Section Three of this book and familiarizing yourself with the comprehensive index of air courier companies. Notice how they are indexed geographically. Select your nearest departure city, then focus on those companies as the ones you will most likely do business with.

Next, phone, write or fax your particular companies of interest and request descriptive literature and application forms. Gather as much information as possible so you will be ready to proceed. Soon, you will be receiving responses back through the mail.

If you do not hear from all of the courier companies of your choice within two weeks. re-contact the missing ones again and re-request the information. Some companies will respond immediately and flood you with helpful information, while other companies will require a little bit of follow-through.

Step three is in parallel with steps one and two, and is the work you will need to do to either apply for a passport, or locate your existing one. Ninety-nine percent of air courier travel is to foreign countries, and a passport is a must. More on passports and visas later.

At this time, you should also check into trip cancellation insurance and medical insurance with your personal insurance company, or others they can refer you to. Keep in mind, that your present medical insurance may only cover you while you are in the United States. You should also inquire into the need for immunization shots. The Center for Disease Control in Atlanta (404-639-3311) or the airline of your choice can assist you with this information.

Soon you will basically be trading your present free time and effort for a substantial cost savings. and a whole new way of travel. Keep in mind that all this preparation is designed to make your first flight as trouble free and rewarding as possible. The expertise you gain from your first air courier adventure will directly build to make your next one, and all the ones to follow, a breeze. As a matter of fact, you will later discover in this book that it's possible for you to travel to exotic destinations on practically a moments notice, for an even less expensive fare! (Sometimes even free!) In the meantime, review all the directions so your first experience will be a happy one.

Now that you have initiated your quest for enthusiasm, begun researching your desired destinations, contemplated "The Big Picture", familiarized yourself with the various air courier companies in Section Three, investigated passports and visas---you are ready to learn more about the mechanics of the air courier field itself.

The main topics which encompass this field are:

- **How Can They Do It?**
- **Courier Vs. Cargo Shipments**
- **Types of Courier Companies**
- **Air Courier Ticket Pricing History**
- **The Basis of Courier Markets**
- **The Future of the Courier Business**
- **Dealing With Booking Agents Vs. Directly With Courier Companies**
- **Rules**
- **Now, Is Courier Travel For You?**

We will now discuss each of these topics in depth.

P
A
R
T

3

BASIC CONCEPTS BEHIND THE AIR COURIER BUSINESS

HOW CAN THEY DO IT?

Surrounding you is an incredible world of commerce! At any given moment around the clock and globe, millions of business deals are being transacted over the phone, fax, by mail, and in person. At any given moment, millions of tons of goods are being transported from everywhere to anywhere as a result of these business deals. Just look around you! You are probably surrounded by countless items which made their way into your life due to either necessity or desire. Tables, chairs, paper, pencils, telephones. typewriters, clocks, lighting fixtures, radios, bags, eating utensils, clothing, books, fans, medical equipment, etc., etc., etc. --- and this is roughly only the top one percent!

Everyone of these items, without exception, had its origin in somebody's mind, and then found its way into this world of materialism by a process called 'invention'. The invention, however, was only the beginning. Clever and aggressive marketing techniques along with an incredible system of distribution and shipping has silently taken its place behind the scenes to make these items available to you in plentiful quantities.

The air courier process is intimately involved in this modern day plethora of consumer goods, and so will be your contribution to the process. To jump ahead a little, let it suffice to say that you may be the courier responsible for carrying a document representing an agreement which soon will have a great worldwide impact, or it could be as simple as a shipment of important consumer goods. In any event, it is safe to say that you will be accompanying articles of great value above the ordinary, simply because of the fact the customers chose to send their goods via the premium air courier option.

Let us now take a look at this 'air courier option'. What is it? Initially, let's look at the basic parameters. Generally speaking, every time a passenger journeys by air to a foreign destination, they are allowed to check-in two bags at no charge in addition to their carry on bag(s). Airlines and rules vary, but for illustration, let's say that each piece of checked luggage can weigh up to forty pounds without an additional charge to the passenger's basic airfare.

Hypothetically, assume for a moment that you have many friends or business contacts who need some parcels delivered to a foreign destination (i.e. Paris) overnight. You certainly couldn't mail these parcels, because that would take a week or two for delivery. A general cargo shipment wouldn't work because cargo takes from three to five days to unload, separate from the container, pass through customs, warehouse, and finally deliver. The only way you could possibly deliver all these parcels for them would be to personally buy an airplane ticket to Paris (approximately $1000), then fill up your suitcases with their parcels and quickly deliver them yourself when you arrive in Paris.

If each parcel weighed approximately one pound, and if you could fit thirty of them in each suitcase (assume the suitcase weighs ten pounds), for a total loaded weight of forty pounds for each suitcase, we could transport sixty, one pound parcels in our two suitcases. The approximate going rate for an overnight delivery service for one pound to a foreign country is an estimated thirty dollars. Multiply $30 x 60 parcels, and you can see that those two previously empty suitcases could earn you $1800! Of course it cost you $1000 for the airplane ticket, and approximately $200 for an overnight hotel, meals, and rental car. If we subtract our $1200 in expenses from our earned $1800, we are left with $600 profit and an opportunity for a Paris holiday.

Unfortunately, not many of us in our spare time can find sixty friends or business contacts needing an overnight delivery service to Paris. Most of us would be lucky if we could find <u>one</u>! This is where the services of an air courier company become apparent.

Air courier companies coordinate the awesome details required to match up cargo needing immediate shipment with individuals willing to fly the trip for a low fare and their checked baggage allowance. Imagine! These air courier companies have their fingers on the pulse beat of volumes of packages needing overnight shipment; they manage the requirements of a pool of people willing to make the trips; coordinate preparation of packages for shipment; arrange the actual airplane ticket purchase with potential couriers such as ourselves; coordinate courier meetings at the departure and arrival airports; facilitate the movement of the goods through customs, and make these goods available to their customers. They also coordinate your return trip home.

It soon becomes apparent that they work very hard for that "$600 profit" we calculated out for our example. This "$600" now is substantially absorbed by the courier's operating expenses (employees, computers, office space, telephone, utilities, etc.). After all these expenses, it would be surprising if they profited close to $100 per shipment when all was said and done. The key to their profit is volume, which in turn opens the door to many flight opportunities for you.

AIR COURIER VS. CARGO SHIPMENTS

In the last portion, we lightly touched on the contrast between air courier and regular cargo shipments. Here we will explain the differences, the advantages, and the disadvantages of each in detail for your broad understanding.

First, we must consider how the international air freight business compares to other means of bulk transportation, such as ocean transport. If we were to take a look at the proportion of each type of shipping means, we would find that the air freight segment accounts for a small percentage of the overall movement of goods in the world. Air courier shipments, in turn, represent a very small proportion when compared to the air freight methods. With this in mind, it is easy to see how air courier shipments are a very specialized class of cargo.

This special class has its special price and advantages. These advantages can best be understood when you consider the realities of shipping via regular air freight. Air freight itself is never accompanied by a passenger during its transit, and as a result, it must meet certain criteria. The cargo itself must arrive at the airport at least five to six hours before departure. Once at the airport, it is packaged/containerized for eventual loading aboard the aircraft.

Upon the aircraft's arrival at its international destination, the air freight containers are off-loaded after all the passengers luggage has been removed from the cargo hold. Then, these air freight containers are transported to a processing facility where they are unloaded, sorted and processed through customs and stored in a bonded warehouse. Next, arrangements are made for eventual pickup by the receiving parties. This process may take as long as a week, before the goods finally reach their destination. In addition, there is a possibility these goods could be lost, stolen, or damaged during this long scenario. As bad as this situation may sound, this method of transportation is still much quicker than an ocean vessel option, but of course much more expensive.

Now, let us compare the premium service of air courier travel to the air freight scenario. Air courier shipping always depends upon a person to accompany the goods on their journey. The first advantage of this air courier method is that the goods may arrive at the airport up until approximately one hour before flight time vs. five hours with air freight. The goods are subsequently loaded aboard the aircraft as the baggage of the accompanying traveler. The aircraft then takes off for its foreign destination as usual, and upon landing, the containers holding the passengers luggage are quickly unloaded so they can be immediately claimed by these passengers.

At that point, a representative from the air courier company arranges all that is necessary to speed these goods through customs and on their way to their awaiting customers. All this can occur within twenty-four hours of the package's journey from the country of origin.

In contrast to the methods of regular air freight, the air courier system offers indisputable speed, reliability, and safety to insure that the goods arrive as expected at their international destination.

As mentioned earlier, the air courier system is a premium service for those individuals which need this speed, reliability, and safety. In accordance with this, the cost is proportional to the increased service for those customers which require it. It is not that air courier service is any "better" than regular air freight, or "better" than ocean vessel transportation, but is simply an alternative mode of transportation which makes sense when customers have certain stringent criteria, and are willing to pay extra for the extra services they require. This is a bonus for us, because we get to accompany these shipments, and see the world at a very low cost!

TYPES OF COURIER COMPANIES

As with practically any business, there are variations in the specific way the business is structured for the particular market. For example, in the world of consumer goods, there exists wholesale, retail, and mail order companies. Within these categories are different levels of service, from warehouse shopping to jewelry stores.

The same type of variations occur within the air courier business, and for your general background they are explained in the next part of this book. For our purposes, we shall discuss five major distinctions under the umbrella of the whole air courier concept. The first four are provided for background information only, and the fifth type is of valuable information to us.

•The first type of air courier business falls under the category of high value item transport (i.e. jewelry/artwork etc.). The cargo transported here is handled by a specialty company such as 'Brinks'. A 'Brinks' type of company needs to have tight control of its couriers for safety and security reasons. Regarding safety, a courier receives special training to safeguard the valuable cargo being accompanied, which is often worth millions of dollars. Regarding security, the courier is bonded and certified as fully trustworthy for the responsibility being assumed for these high value goods. In accordance with the above two factors, it is extremely important this type of company only assign fully trained, accountable and protected personnel on their air courier routes. Generally, free-lance couriers such as you and I are not qualified for these positions without extensive special training. This training can only be provided by the air courier company itself.

• The next type of air courier company is an operation which is mostly 'self contained' (i.e. UPS), meaning they operate many of their own package pickup and delivery vehicles, along with their own aircraft. Their personnel handle, process, and expedite most of the packages through the entire transit process. This type of company rarely admits to directly needing assistance from on board couriers like ourselves.

• The third type of courier service specializes in finding customers for large courier types of operations. This kind of courier company earns its money by 'selling' huge quantities of packages, at quantity discount prices to these large air courier operations. They are mostly concerned with finding goods for shipping, and they in turn forward these goods to these large courier companies, who generally operate many of their own aircraft and ground transportation vehicles. These companies generally do not utilize the services of free-lance air courier personnel.

• The fourth type of courier operation is the kind which is integral within an occasional company (generally a larger one). You might say that these couriers are staff people who function as a courier, but also have other responsibilities within their company when they are not flying. This type of operation is usually not of particular interest to free-lance couriers. However, if you are interested in this type of employment, we suggest that you individually contact those possible corporations which may be of interest to you.

•The last type of courier service is of great interest to us. This particular operation is responsible for a large coordination effort which focuses on: 1) Finding willing couriers, such as ourselves. 2) Integrating the shipments of various package collection sources, and, in accordance with the quantity of goods, reserve flight space. 3) Negotiating the airfares with the airlines based upon volume. 4) Working with other courier companies on a reciprocal nature, and coordinate meetings with air courier company representatives at the origin and destination airports as efficiency dictates.

Because no two air courier companies have the same composition or structure, it is very likely that they could be made up from a little bit of each of the above five operating philosophies.

AIR COURIER TICKET PRICING HISTORY

Just a word now about the history of how air courier companies have evolved the pricing structure which will determine your applicable airfare.

In the early days, shortly after the advent of jet transportation, it was somewhat common for an air courier company to cover the cost of the free-lance courier's airplane ticket, along with hotel and spending money. Times and circumstances have changed, and so has this policy. The airfare is no longer free, the per diem has stopped, and so has the payment for lodging at the courier's destination. All this for a combination of reasons.

The first factor was the occasional lack of a courier's reliability, which would strand the air courier company with a shipment that could only be completed by an employee, or a last minute volunteer. The air courier companies then discovered there were people willing to pay a reduced rate for a dream journey the courier company could regularly offer. At this time, the free tickets and many benefits began to disappear.

Air courier travel is still a good deal today for both parties because the courier companies experience a very low frequency of last minute cancellations (as the courier will generally forfeit the cost of their ticket), and the fares are still low enough to be a great bargain. More about fares and agreements later on in this book.

THE BASIS OF COURIER MARKETS

Earlier, we discussed the worldwide plethora of consumer goods, and how business deals are constantly underway perpetuating the consumer industry's growth.

Millions of business centers, large and small, interact daily. Telephone calls, telefaxes and meetings occur amongst interested parties, and as a result, countless goods are shipped between these centers of commerce.

Most of us are familiar with the common methods of shipping goods within the United States. Organizations such as the United States Postal Service, United Parcel Service, Federal Express, various air freight and trucking companies, etc. offer a wide range of services from overnight to week-long delivery.

The many delivery options in the United States practically guarantee that any interested individual can ship almost any class of goods country-wide for a low cost, at a moments notice. As a result of the large number of these reliable options, the services of an air courier company are rarely needed within these United States.

Fortunately for us, the shipment of special goods between international destinations is not nearly as mature or efficient as the common shipping services offered within the United States for non-special goods. In order for special international shipments to even approximate the level of proficiency and speed within the United States, the requirement for our services as 'International Free-Lance Air Couriers' is very real.

Take a look at the consumer goods which surround you. Aside from those items which are obviously American, you will notice that a great quantity of these other goods come from locations such as the Far East and Europe. Evidently the business arrangements were made between locations throughout the United States and these international centers of commerce. Certain deeply entrenched trading routes (some hundreds of years old) are the key to the most likely prospects for abundant air courier services.

Through established gateways flow indescribable amounts of goods per hour, around the clock. Out of the nature of so many goods being moved, it is logical to assume that the variations of goods will require different levels of attention, service and speed. The complications of customs, warehousing, etc. encountered by international air freight may not be acceptable for certain classes of goods, and only articles accompanied by an air courier stand a chance of rapid processing and delivery.

Examples of highly traveled courier routes are: New York to most of Europe (i.e. Amsterdam, Brussels, London, Milan, Paris, Zurich, etc.); New York to South America (i.e. Buenos Aries, Rio, etc.); and New York to the Orient (i.e. Hong Kong, Singapore, Tokyo).

Other major gateways to similar destinations are Miami, Chicago, Houston, Los Angeles, and San Francisco. For an accurate update on these main departure points, and the courier companies which presently serve them, be sure to follow through with your inquiries of the courier companies in Chapter Three which interest you, as suggested earlier in this book.

THE FUTURE OF THE AIR COURIER BUSINESS

You are now hopefully acquiring a strong understanding of what the air courier business is all about. In accordance with this new-found knowledge, your enthusiasm and anticipation for your first journey should be growing.

By looking at the air courier business of the past, we will now attempt to project an accurate picture of its future. From this viewpoint, you will gain an appreciation of the possible opportunities which await you.

The courier business has changed little in its long meaningful history. About the only dramatic changes are the vehicles of transport. One can hardly compare a month long ocean journey to a five hour airplane flight between the same points!

In the last ten years, inventions such as the fax machine have really taken commercial hold. Although the use of these fax machines is extensive, they have not caused any negative impact upon the air courier business, which has grown by leaps and bounds through this time. All Available information indicates that this should not change in the foreseeable future. As a rule, it is easy to understand that documents longer than approximately thirty pages would cost more in international long distance charges and labor to fax, than to simply send by an air courier.

Most important documents, such as a contract, often requires a timely signature to close a deal. To simply mail an important contract back and forth across an ocean may take an unacceptable period of time, not to mention the risks involved. To have an individual make an international journey to only sign their name would probably be a prohibitive option, so here again we can readily see how an air courier service is the most cost effective and rapid solution.

An un-faxable object needing rapid international delivery is a prime candidate for delivery by an air courier service. This truth is bound to remain constant until that one future day when every interested businessman owns a 'Star Trek' type transporter system. As far-fetched as this seems, imagine the look on a pony express rider's face if you were to inform him that just over one hundred years after his last ride, there would be jet aircraft carrying mail at close to the speed of sound. Or if you wish, you could impress this fellow by telling him how an object known as a telefax machine can deliver a letter across the United States, door to door, in less than a minute. Then, tell him that this delivery machine is a very common consumer item!

Still, despite all the amazing and wonderful inventions bound to come our way in the future, it is a safe bet to say that in the meantime, you will have the opportunity to travel the world many times over very inexpensively as an air courier.
Other factors, which indicate that the air courier system is here to stay, are reflected in the ever growing and changing patterns of international trade. In the past few years we have all been privileged to witness dramatic world changes around the globe. Most of these changes add up to increased possibilities for New World Trade.

Correspondingly, the demand for air couriers to new destinations, such as Moscow, will probably be a natural part of this expansion, as the quantity of goods being shipped constantly increases.

So, pack your bags and get ready to go! If air courier travel seems to interest you from what you've read so far, be prepared to embark upon a lifetime of international exploration in your spare time.

DEALING WITH BOOKING AGENTS VS. DIRECTLY WITH COURIER COMPANIES

Until now, we have mainly dealt with general concepts to afford you a solid foundation about the air courier business. In this segment, we will focus on the specifics needed to get yourself actually started. Are you ready?

Earlier, we had suggested that you familiarize yourself with all the air courier companies listed in Section Three, and begin contacting them immediately for information. The first thing we will asses is whether these businesses are actual air courier companies, or entities known as 'booking agents'. You may be asking yourself what the difference is, so we will now explain.

As previously mentioned, a very large air courier company regularly performs most of their operations internally, and requires very little outside support. At the other end of the spectrum, there are small organizations which only specialize in a particular aspect of operations, and they regularly work in conjunction with other courier companies to provide a complete service. Included in this, and somewhere in-between, are the courier companies which specialize only in the packaging and transport segment, while often times leaving the booking of air courier passengers to another organization. These other organizations are called 'booking agents'.

A booking agent is often an official 'go between' representing single or multiple air courier companies. Their services are generally helpful, especially to beginning air couriers. A large booking agent such as '**Now Voyager**' in New York represents multiple courier companies, and can generally offer you a greater assortment of destinations and flight times than a single courier company only representing themselves.

One of the greatest benefits of a booking agency is their willingness to bend over backwards by working very closely with you, and by answering all of your questions. They are highly motivated to do all they can to secure your services, as they only earn their money when they sell a seat.

Some booking agents offer extra assistance such as a message line. This message line serves to keep the couriers advised of future flight opportunities. In some cases, the booking agents will work with you to secure an inexpensive domestic flight between your local city and the courier flight's departure airport.

The survival of a booking agent depends upon how well they serve the air couriers such as you and I, and their shipping agency customers. Therefore, you can generally be sure that their level of service to you will be high, and that they will be constantly tracking the pulse beat of the industry to have information of interest readily available for you.

Of course, the extra benefits of a booking agency usually come at some price. The most common form is a yearly membership fee, which may be worth it if you take a number of trips per year. You will have to be the judge of the tradeoffs for yourself. A booking agent may earn some additional compensation for their extra services by minimally increasing the fare of a ticket. Again, you will have to be the judge as to whether the extra money you might pay is worth it for your unique circumstances.

In contrast to the booking agents, dealing directly with the courier companies themselves has its advantages. Mainly, you are closer to the source of the action. By this, we mean the courier company's staff, who will probably get to know you well after a few of your journeys. At that point, they will probably become as friendly and helpful to you as a booking agent initially is. The big difference here however, is that you will not be paying any membership fees or ticket surcharges for this extra level of attention.

Another reason you may choose to deal directly with an actual air courier company vs. a booking agency is that some air courier companies may be flying a route only offered by them. This simply means that a particular destination may not be available any other way.

Booking agent vs. air courier company, which will it be? Before you make your decision, be sure to have all the facts, and weigh them against your personal needs.

RULES

As with anything of importance in life, the greater the amount of responsibility you can demonstrate, the greater will be your freedom and rewards. In your role as an on board air courier, there are no exceptions to this concept.

Think about it! When you fly for an air courier company, you are personally escorting people's prized documents and possessions, most having a very high intrinsic value. These customers have selected the most costly form of international package transportation available, and have silently put their trust in your abilities to do your part to insure success.

The overall key to your success is integral with conducting yourself in the most professional, and responsible manner possible when flying as an air courier. Now for the specific details as to what is meant by this.

Your responsibilities begin when the air courier company signs a contract with you for your services in exchange for the substantial travel discount you'll receive. This contract is a very meaningful document, and should be read thoroughly.

Punctuality is exceedingly important. When the air courier company asks you to be at their office or airport at a specific time, be there! This is one of the easiest ways for you to enhance your reputation and personal image with them. Remember! The better your reputation and image, the better positioned you will be for special considerations in the future.

As far as 'how to dress', always take a conservative attitude until such time that you can make an informed decision to do otherwise. When you finally select your first air courier company to fly with, be sure you fully understand their dress guidelines. If you have any doubts or questions, be sure to ask if they are fully enforcing their criteria at this time. In general, you will find that most air courier companies only ask that you not dress outrageously, and that your neat appearance contributes to enforcing their professional reputation. Remember! The better you look, the better they will look!

Consuming any alcohol in conjunction with your journey is generally prohibited. Please understand that the air courier company is only trying to insure that they deliver their goods as promised to the customer. If, out of the thousands of air couriers who fly each year, they can eliminate that one case where someone would not have met their obligations due to intoxication, their alcohol control program has earned its weight in gold.

Intoxication may cause loss or delay of a shipment worth perhaps millions of dollars, resulting in a catastrophic situation for all concerned parties. You may ask "How could an individual cause such a chain of negative events if intoxicated?" Answers to this question follow.

First of all, you must take the flight you are booked on, since you and your ticket are matched up to the goods checked aboard that particular flight. If you aren't aboard, the airline's baggage cross reference won't allow the goods to be carried aboard that aircraft. If those goods aren't shipped as scheduled, there will be some very unhappy people waiting on the receiving end, not to mention the people who thought they were shipping the goods at a certain time. Simply put, if you find yourself enjoying some drinking activity in the bar at the departure airport as your flight silently pulls away, you will have some very unhappy consequences attached to that particular event.

Another drawback to being intoxicated during the pre-departure stage is that you will be carrying a large envelope containing information regarding the goods you are accompanying. If you were to accidentally leave this envelope behind anywhere, you would also be in 'deep trouble'! Can you picture trying to explain to the courier representative meeting you at your destination that you accidentally left your envelope behind at your originating airport in the bar, bathroom, or departure lounge because of carelessness enhanced by intoxication!

Once aboard and flying, this envelope is your personal responsibility. During the entire trip you are not allowed to tamper with it in any way, or let it out of your control. Simply put, you are doing a simple, but extremely important job.

When you arrive at your destination, and the courier representative greeting you says your work is complete, you are then on your own. The only things you will need to keep in mind at this time are your responsibilities for the return journey. Be sure that you leave yourself enough sober time to fully meet these responsibilities.

When functioning in an on board courier status, most companies ask that you keep your arrangements with them confidential. To find out what your particular company requires, be sure to read your contract and ask lots of questions, if necessary.

If you are fortunate enough to arrange for your courier flight on board an airline with which you have a **frequent flier membership**, you are really **in for a bonus!** On one long round trip, you could earn close to enough miles for a free domestic ticket!

There are so many ways that air courier travel can enhance and change your life. If you follow the air courier company's common sense rules, everybody wins. You will build a great reputation of professional responsibility, which will attract even greater opportunities your way.

NOW, IS COURIER TRAVEL FOR YOU?

By now, you should have a fairly good feeling that you will enjoy being on board as an air courier. Don't forget, once you pay for your ticket, you are usually committed. It is therefore imperative, that you feel good about the adventure you are about to take. We will now help you firm up your understanding of the opportunities available to you, by presenting different points of view on the typical realities involved with being an on board air courier.

Most courier trips require one to two weeks, and these schedules are generally rigid. If you simply do not have enough vacation time for this typical length of stay, you will have to do further research to locate courier companies who have trips of shorter time durations.

Next, you will need to decide on the most convenient/cost-effective way to get from your hometown to the courier departure airport. Practically all air courier flights depart from New York, Miami, Los Angeles, San Francisco, Houston, and Chicago. Let's say that you live in Wyoming, and your closest gateway city is San Francisco. You might have to schedule an additional few days for the round trip drive to San Francisco, and you'll have to add in the cost of food and lodging along the way. Also, don't forget to account for the parking fees when you leave your car at or near the San Francisco Airport. An alternative to driving would be for you to find an inexpensive round trip flight from your home town airport to San Francisco. A few courier companies may even help you locate such a flight, so be sure to at least ask them. You'll need to consider the costs involved with transporting yourself to the courier departure airport, in addition to the cost of the courier flight itself. You will usually find that the total cost will be substantially lower than the total 'through' cost would have been with a non-courier flight.

Another aspect of the air courier business is that some popular destinations may have seasonal availabilities. By this we mean that it may be easier to secure a flight to Paris in the winter than in the summer. If you plan ahead, then book and pay early, you will usually have the greatest number of flight destinations to choose from.

Now, we will briefly discuss baggage allowance. As stated earlier, you are being provided with a very low cost international ticket, in exchange for some concessions on your part. Probably the most noticeable concession is the restriction on baggage you can take with you. Although rules vary from airline to airline, and courier to courier, let's say, for demonstration sake, that you are only allowed one carry-on bag, and no checked baggage. In general, don't forget that the lighter the load you fly with, the lesser the load you will have to carry around at your destination. Also, keep in mind that you will probably be purchasing some goods during your journey, and you will need room to pack them for the return trip. To say the least, you will want to fully understand and feel comfortable with the baggage requirements inherent with being an air courier. Starting on page 73, we will fully address the guidelines of baggage allowance.

For those of you who find traveling alone agreeable, you will probably enjoy the feeling of freedom inherent in this venture. If you must travel with a friend or loved one, you can have them purchase a regular inexpensive ticket on your flight, find another air courier company flying the same flight, or have your partner try to book another courier flight during the same general time frame. Rarely will a single air courier company book two seats on the same aircraft, as they will usually process additional baggage onto your single ticket by simply paying extra fees for that additional baggage. These additional fees are still much less expensive than buying another ticket for an additional courier.

As a potential on board air courier, it is important that you exercise patience and understanding when working with the air courier company. While the air courier company naturally wants to fulfill your expectations for a great trip, flights to your desired destination, at your requested time, simply may not be available. You might have to change your desired destination, or departure time, if you are to indeed book a journey.

The chances are 99-1/2% that your trip will be completed originally as planned. However, once a journey is booked, there is a very slight possibility the air courier company might re-assign your services to a different flight or destination at the last minute. They can do this because the airplane ticket you are holding is not really yours; it is theirs, with your name on it. Simply put, you are not the one that arranged to ship all those goods you are accompanying; the air courier company did. The money you paid for your ticket is legally an administrative fee. To learn more about the specifics, read and understand your contract completely, and ask questions if you don't understand.

If you are one of those rare individuals who is switched at the last minute, there are two ways you can react to it. The first is with a great sense of adventure, and the second is with a lesser sense of adventure. In either event, there are probably going to be some outstanding experiences awaiting you on your journey.

Once you arrive at your international destination, always keep in mind that your return date, time, and flight are fixed entities unless the courier company needs to administer some unlikely last minute change.

The bottom line is that being an on board air courier will save you many dollars, and provide you the opportunity to see parts of the world you probably would not have seen otherwise. Along with this incredible opportunity, are the accompanying minor restrictions and drawbacks. Don't forget, even a first class, full fare ticket on the Concorde has its restrictions.

The name of the game is 'get involved', and with this involvement you will position yourself for unbelievable travel opportunities. Think of the air courier company as your friend and co-worker, and try to treat them as such. If you have just experienced a fantastic adventure, send a thank-you note to the head of the air courier company. The more reliable and considerate you are of them, the more benefits they will return to you. How many people can say they have 'a friend' that practically guarantees them opportunities for very low cost international travel? As incredible as it seems, right now they are waiting for you to make yourself known, and give them a hand!

SECTION
TWO

HOW TO START

In Section Two, we will walk you through all the steps necessary to successfully board the aircraft for your air courier journey. We will assume here that you have followed all the steps outlined in Section One of this book, and that you have a growing understanding of what lies ahead for you as an air courier.

The first thing you will need to do is verify that you meet the air courier's minimum age requirement, which is usually between eighteen and twenty-one years. If you think this may concern you, discuss it with the particular courier companies that interest you.

Once this initial step is complete, you will definitely need to secure a passport. If you already have a passport, make approximately ten copies of it and put them in a file at home for later mailing to air courier companies wanting proof of your passport. A small accordion type file will help you organize all your courier papers, and will be an invaluable tool for you to use during your career as an air courier.

Now, let's talk about visas. If your air courier travels involve visits to countries requiring visas, you will need to get this important documentation in order too. A reliable list of countries requiring visas is available from the:

CONSUMER INFORMATION CENTER
PUEBLO, CO 81009
ATTN: DEPT. 438T, 'FOREIGN VISA REQUIREMENTS'

Once you have all your visa information in hand, make a few copies of it so you can send it along to the air courier company for proof, if and when necessary. Generally, the air courier company will want to maintain an up-to-date file on you and the countries you have immediate access to visit. Therefore, it's in your best interest to let them know you are practically ready to go anywhere, at anytime. Visas are usually inexpensive, easy to obtain, and good for several months or years.

As far as your personal courier file is concerned, keep abreast of any official travel advisory by calling the:

DEPARTMENT OF STATE HOTLINE FOR TRAVEL ADVISORIES
202-647-5225

The information you receive from them can give you an official accurate status on the country you wish to visit, at any time. In addition to this travel advisory information, the hotline can assist you with passport information, etc.

As a last helpful hint here, it is a good idea for you take a photocopy of your passport along on your journey (in case you lose your official passport while traveling, this copy will facilitate in getting a quick replacement), and also take a couple of extra official photographs of yourself for quickly obtaining additional visas if they are necessary while you are abroad.

Well, we are about ready to start calling air courier companies to gather information on booking our first trip! By now you should have selected approximately three destination choices, and have done some research on these places. You will have also studied all the information the courier companies sent back to you about themselves, and hopefully you have picked roughly three of these companies you think will best suit your needs.

The key to great opportunities with an air courier company lies in the flexibility of your schedule and agenda. By giving the courier companies various options on how to serve you, you will have the greatest chances for rewarding travel.

The best way to inform any air courier company that you are indeed flexible, is to exercise one or more of the following specific options. These approaches are very valuable when practiced in place of, or in addition to, the standard approach of requesting precise dates, times, and destinations.

<u>Approach Number One</u>: Pick a time slot when you know you will be free to take a vacation. For example purposes, let's select September 1 through 14. With this time slot in mind, tell the air courier company that you are willing to travel to any destination they may have available within those two weeks. They will probably offer you a few selections, and one of these may be one of your primary choices anyway! This approach will leave the air courier company with the impression you are a very flexible person, and this may very well contribute towards positioning yourself as a future 'preferred customer' of this particular air courier company.

<u>Approach Number Two</u>: Decide upon your specific destination, or destinations, and a general time slot

you will be available for travel (i.e. the month of July). Present this information to the air courier company in the following manner: "I am free during the entire month of July to travel to Paris, Milan, or London. What is available at your least expensive fare during this time frame?"

They will then pick out some specific dates, and hopefully one or more of your destinations as an option. If the total package sounds good to you, you have both come up winners. The air courier company will begin to see you as a flexible, good natured customer, and they will be very likely to remember your virtues in the future.

Now it's time to take stock of where you are. Do you have a passport in hand? Will you choose a booking agent to work with, or will you work directly with an air courier company? Will you have to pay any kind of membership fee? If so, do you think it will be worth it? Will you have any special situations to consider when it comes time to get to a departure airport (i.e. How close do you live to the probable departure airport?)?

If you feel that you did well in getting to this point (without actually purchasing your ticket yet), congratulations! You have taken your initial steps into a realm unknown to most people.

MAKING ARRANGEMENTS

It is now time to start integrating and applying all the background you have acquired, so you can confidently deal with an air courier company to actually book your flight. Assuming you have made a 'dry run' or two speaking with some courier companies during your information gathering stage, you are basically familiar with what to expect when they answer their telephone.

Are you ready to commit some of your hard earned money to one of these courier flight opportunities? If so, there are a few things you'll need to keep in mind as you make your reservation. The courier company, like any other company, can only survive if they make a profit. This means that they are very anxious to secure your reservation and payment as soon as possible. Your payment is very significant to them, no matter how small it is.

For payment, policies differ between air courier companies. While some may require a simple personal check mailed in for a deposit, others may require a cashier's check hand delivered or express mailed to them. Some may have the convenience of a credit card option for the deposit/full payment, but possibly may charge you a fee for that convenience. You will simply have to discuss the particular payment options and rules with the air courier company you are dealing with.

Costs can vary for a particular destination at a particular time, on a particular flight. By this we mean the cost for a seat can range between full regular air courier fare (still very inexpensive), and no cost at all! There is a philosophy behind this variance that you should always keep in mind when securing your flight. We shall explain that philosophy next.

When an air courier company books flights, they will generally reserve seats up to approximately three months in advance of the departure date. This time varies, but we will use three months for illustration. Let's put our feet in the air courier company's shoes, and see how they operate. We will also take a look at what makes them feel comfortable, and what makes them nervous.

Let us suppose we would like to depart on our journey in approximately two and one half months. There is a great chance we will get a fairly good selection of destinations, because not too many people have booked flights yet. Accordingly, the courier company will probably quote you a 'higher fare', as they aren't too concerned right now about filling that flight opportunity which is so far in the future. If you choose not to get the ticket, they still have ample time to fill that seat. It is all a matter of demand. You are trading a few extra dollars for the relative certainty that you will get to go where you want, when you want!

Now, in the opposite situation, suppose they have a flight scheduled to depart in two days, and a designated air courier had to cancel because of an emergency. Even though the courier passenger probably had to forfeit most or all of the payment, the air courier company is presently without a courier for that flight. The courier company could send an employee on this trip to cover the emergency (and lose that employee's productivity for a few days), or they could book someone who called up at the last minute to ask "What destinations are available within the next week?" The air courier company will probably respond something like this: "We have a trip available in two days from Los Angeles to Tokyo, then back to Los Angeles seven days later. The round trip fare is eighty dollars. Are you interested?" Now, despite the fact that the air courier company had to expend time and effort to address this problem (a last minute intense administrative re-arrangement, to say the least), you might be wondering how and why they would let this trip go for such an inexpensive fare.

First of all, remember that they probably will retain the payment from the first courier who had to cancel, so the ticket is basically paid for. Next, and probably the most important point (that you must always keep in mind), is that if a courier flight is available anywhere close to flight time, it usually means that the air courier company is in a bind, and can't take any chances of missing the flight opportunity for their planned shipment. Their posture will therefore be to place someone on that flight immediately, even if it means selling the seat at a very low fare, or even giving it away at no charge.

In accordance with these extremes, you have a variety of choices to pursue: Book far in advance when you have the greatest opportunity for securing exactly the flight you want, or, wait until a couple of days before and 'see how you can help them out of a tough spot'. Of course, there is always the in-between time frames of roughly one to one and one half months prior to departure which would command prices which are in-between the normal, and ridiculously low amounts. If you live in a major gateway city with many air courier companies, you can experiment with different approaches and see which works the best for you.

Once your flight planning is complete and you have secured a reservation, you will probably need to sign a contract, if you haven't done so already. Together with your passport, visa (if necessary), and your deposit/full payment etc., you are now 'practically in the system and ready to go'. Congratulations on making it this far!

YOUR PART OF THE AGREEMENT

The air courier company you selected is now poised to fulfill their part of the agreement to send you on your way. Your part of the agreement is just as vital as theirs, and we shall now discuss highlights of the very important ways you can successfully fulfill your requirements in a most satisfactory manner.

Earlier, we discussed the great importance of demonstrating your abilities of professionalism and responsibility towards the air courier company you chose to work with. Please re-read that section on the importance of reliability, promptness, how to dress, and alcohol policy. (See 'Rules' page 45).

Your positive image is your most important asset! To put it plainly, if your reputation is less than acceptable, word will get around between air courier companies via sources which commonly service many of these companies. If that occurs, you will most likely have a very difficult time being accepted for future opportunities within the air courier industry.

A very important concept touched upon earlier was your responsibility for the envelope you will carry containing the manifests (lists) of the goods you are accompanying on your journey. Always have that envelope under your control! Never surrender it to anyone who hasn't proven to you beyond a shadow of a doubt, that they are the individual authorized to receive it.

Make sure you thoroughly understand the contract you have committed yourself to with the air courier company. Typically, this contract will describe all the aspects of eligibility, responsibilities, liability, ticketing, baggage allowance, payment, deposit, and cancellation.

With all this information in mind, and understood, you can rest assured that there will be little left to chance when the time comes for you to 'sign on the bottom line'.

YOUR BAGGAGE ALLOWANCE

The amount of personal baggage you can take on a courier flight is often a challenge to your packing abilities. You will generally be limited to only one piece of carry-on luggage, and perhaps a second small piece. Ask your courier company if they strictly enforce their blanket luggage rule, and also ask the airline what their policy is. If they differ, discuss this with the courier company.

The 'baggage' the air courier company checks in your name will probably never be seen by you, and you are absolutely not responsible for its contents. If someone is attempting to ship illegal material on your manifest, they will be held responsible, not you.

You and your personal luggage will be searched by customs however, so remember that you are totally responsible for all your personal possessions, the air courier company is not!

If you feel greatly restricted by the standard baggage limitations, you may be pleased to know that there are a number of ways to take along a few extra items.

We will now discuss five practical ideas:

The first approach is to wear a few layers of clothing prior to departure, and remove them once aboard. This especially works well if you have a bulky sweater or jacket which would ordinarily take up a great percentage of your luggage space if packed. Once aboard, you can simply stow the extra garments, then put them back on when you arrive.

The second idea is to have a light bag type suitcase packed inside your official carry-on bag that you can access once aboard. When convenient, and only if there is room, place these layers of clothing in that suitcase, and stow it along with your official bag. From that point on, and through your entire trip, utilize this suitcase just like the other one until it is time to come home. At that point, just before departure, put your layers back on, and stuff the bag type suitcase back inside your official carry-on.

The next suggestion for getting around the baggage restriction is more of a long-shot, but may be helpful to you. This possibility rests in the chance that you may be accompanying only one checked parcel on your courier trip. If that is the case, there just may be an opportunity for one of your personal bags to be checked as the other parcel, at probably no cost to you. Unfortunately, the courier company probably won't know until close to departure time if this possibility exists, and by then it will probably be too late for you to plan accordingly. If you think that you could adapt quickly to this last minute opportunity, by all means investigate it. Keep in mind however, that if you are functioning as a

68

courier on the flight home, chances are very slim that you would have this opportunity again. You would then be in the position of checking this bag for an additional fee, if the courier company has no objections. Be sure to discuss this whole scenario with the air courier company before committing yourself to this option.

The fourth suggestion is a bit different from the previous ones. It involves departing on your journey with a carry-on bag which is practically empty. Why would you want to do this? First of all, you will breeze through customs upon your international arrival, but that is not our primary intention here. The real reason is to free up your luggage space for a possible bargain shopping spree!

Let's estimate that you saved approximately four-hundred to six-hundred dollars on your airfare by traveling as an air courier. Now, add to the equation that you are allowed to bring up to four-hundred dollars of foreign purchases into the United States duty-free when you arrive back home. If you decide to purchase a few articles of quality expensive clothing overseas, keep in mind that this same clothing would probably sell for many times the price in the United States. Plainly put, those four-hundred dollars worth of duty-free goods could cost you as much as two thousand dollars if purchased here in the United States! Just think about it! You go on a dream vacation, and fill you closet with some quality clothing you needed anyway. All this for the price of what would have been only the cost of a non-courier type discount ticket!

In other words (example for illustration only):

$400 (Courier Ticket) + $400 (Duty Free Purchases) = $800
vs
$2,000 (Typical cost of the same goods if bought in U.S.)

From the above example, you can easily see how taking that dream vacation can very possibly save you many dollars.

We hope this discussion on baggage allowance served to help you find ways to adapt to the possible inconveniences you might have to face at flight time. For those of you who would normally never pack more than a small carry-on bag, we hope that the shopping approach just illustrated will be of some interest to you.

Of course, there is always this fifth and last alternative available if you wish to travel home as empty as possible: Have your extra baggage shipped back by a freight company or the postal service. This approach will reunite your goods with you in only a few short weeks.

TICKETING PROCEDURES AND CHECK-IN/FLYING AND ARRIVING/RETURNING

TICKETING PROCEDURES AND CHECK-IN

Now that the 'big day' has almost arrived, you will need to <u>confirm your travel intentions</u> with the courier company. This is done by calling them during the time frame they specified in your contract. If for some reason you forget to call, there is a chance that your reservation will be canceled, and you will forfeit your payment and trip. Also, the air courier company will certainly note your lack of responsibility.

On the day of your flight, you will need to meet a representative of the air courier company at the airport, or at another location, as specified by them. Be sure to take the courier company's telephone number with you to the airport, so you can call their office if there is a last minute mix-up. <u>Do not</u> leave the specified meeting location, or call the courier company unless it seems very certain that the representative will not show up in time for you to get on your flight.

The representative may be late due to possible manifest changes on your ticket. Often times, additional parcels will trickle in right up until the last minute, and the courier company will want to accommodate them. Usually, the courier company's shipment is the last of the goods loaded aboard the aircraft, so they can have a final opportunity to make these last minute changes.

The possible tardiness of the air courier representative does not provide <u>you</u> with the right to be late. We suggest that you be patient, and realize that any possible minor inconvenience is a small price to pay for your deeply discounted travel.

When the courier representative meets you, you will: Receive your long awaited airplane ticket; be assisted with check-in; be given the manifest envelope and baggage receipts for the courier company to claim the shipment at your destination (more about that later); and you will be given a very important instruction sheet describing the procedures for your return flight. Safeguard this instruction sheet, and if possible, make a second copy of it in case the original is lost.

This entire check-in process is a great opportunity for you to see a piece of the air courier business in action. If you get along well with the representative who meets you, use this opportunity to ask any questions you may have about the air courier business. You just might get some exciting inside information that could set your next trip in motion!

FLYING AND ARRIVING

Well, you are aboard the aircraft now, and in your seat. All your concerns about getting to this point are history. While flying, be sure you maintain control over the manifest envelope, your important documents, and those baggage claim receipts.

Now you have landed, and your dream trip is coming alive! Before you go bounding out of the airport in amazement, remember that you still have a very important obligation to fulfill.

Per the air courier company's instructions, you will meet the courier representative who is awaiting your arrival. As soon as your identities are confirmed, you will need to hand over the manifest pouch and the baggage claim receipts. You will then be asked to wait a short time while your shipment clears customs. Once this is complete, you are free to go. Have fun!!!

RETURNING

Your trip is now winding down, and it is time to pull out that instruction sheet you tucked away at the beginning of your journey. Most likely, the instruction sheet states you must call the courier company approximately twenty-four hours before departure. You must do this, lest you falter in your image of professionalism. Also, it is important to note that this telephone call is much more than a formality, and the conversation may reveal a last minute change of flight plan, or some other important information. At a minimum, your phone call confirms to the courier company that you are poised to make the return trip home as planned.

If you are not familiar with the public telephone system of the country you are visiting, be sure you have time to figure it out in order to successfully make this important confirmation call.

SPECIAL SITUATIONS

So far, we have covered the common situations you are bound to encounter as an on board air courier traveler.

One must be prepared for occasional ways of doing business which are different from ways one is used to. When functioning as a courier, you will encounter different courier check-in and arrival procedures at the vastly different airports you will visit. Always be sure you totally understand these unique procedures before you arrive in a situation where you will have to perform correctly.

Strive to be open to the possibility that the unpredicted situation you may suddenly find yourself in, could have a greater reward than the planned situation you envisioned.

Be patient, read and understand your contract, ask questions whenever you can, think ahead, and have a great time!

SECTION
THREE

COURIER COMPANY CONTACTS

The following pages contain a comprehensive listing of air courier companies for you to contact.

This section is arranged like a typical airline schedule, with the departure city listed at the heading, and the destinations following alphabetically.

The departure cities are listed in order of the number of destinations presently served, with London totaling 36, New York 24, Miami 17, Los Angeles 12, San Francisco 5, Houston 2, Montreal 2, Toronto 2, Vancouver, B.C. 1 and Chicago 1.

In an airline schedule, they list departure and arrival times along with flight numbers. Here, we only list the air courier companies for your reference, as it would be impossible for us to specify airlines, flight numbers and times, due to the constant changes in the air courier and airline industry.

Following the 'airline schedule' type listing, we have provided the addresses and telephone numbers of all the air courier companies in the geographical order they were referred to.

Don't forget that changing patterns in the air courier industry can cause route changes almost overnight. Therefore, if the listing of available destinations does not indicate a routing you are very interested in, be sure to ask each and every air courier company you deal with if they 'by chance' have begun flying, or will begin flying, to this destination of your desire. You never know what tomorrow will bring in the air courier business, so take every opportunity to insure that you may be able to get to the place you want to go to as an air courier.

We recommend that you keep a separate dedicated notebook for recording information the air courier company will give you in the course of your discussions. Always be prepared to ask them about any recent changes in policy, in addition to possible questions about recent destination additions or deletions. Be sure to ask them about the range of discounts you can expect with varied booking times, and if they deeply discount or ever give away free flights on short notice. If they do, ask them what their procedure is for listing yourself as a possible resource for them to call upon when these free, or almost free flights become available.

DESTINATIONS AVAILABLE FROM NEW YORK, NEW YORK

NEW YORK TO AMSTERDAM, NETHERLANDS

Courier Travel Service
Discount Travel International
Halbart Express
Now Voyager

NEW YORK TO BRUSSELS, BELGIUM

Courier Travel Service
Discount Travel International
Halbart Express
Now Voyager

NEW YORK TO BUENOS ARIES, ARGENTINA

Air Facility
Courier Travel Service
Discount Travel International
Now Voyager

NEW YORK TO CARACAS, VENEZUELA

Air Facility
Courier Travel Service
Discount Travel International
Now Voyager

NEW YORK TO COPENHAGEN, DENMARK

Courier Travel Service
Discount Travel International
Halbart Express
Now Voyager

NEW YORK TO FRANKFURT, GERMANY

Courier Travel Service
Discount Travel International
Halbart Express
Now Voyager

NEW YORK TO GENEVA, SWITZERLAND

Now Voyager

NEW YORK TO HONG KONG

Courier Travel Service
Discount Travel International
Jupiter Air, Ltd. (Micom America, Inc.)
Now Voyager

NEW YORK TO LONDON, ENGLAND

Able Travel and Tours
Courier Travel and Tours
Discount Travel International
Halbart Express
Intermail Courier
Now Voyager
Priority Air Freight NY, Ltd.

NEW YORK TO MADRID, SPAIN

Courier Travel Service
Discount Travel International
Halbart Express
Now Voyager

NEW YORK TO MANILA, PHILIPPINES

East-West Express

NEW YORK TO MEXICO CITY, MEXICO

Discount Travel International
Now Voyager
World Courier, Inc.

NEW YORK TO MILAN, ITALY

Courier Travel Service
Discount Travel International
Halbart Express
Now Voyager

NEW YORK TO MONTEVIDEO, URUGUAY

Air Facility
Courier Travel Service
Discount Travel International

NEW YORK TO PARIS, FRANCE

Able Travel and Tours
Courier Travel Service
Discount Travel International
Halbart Express
Now Voyager

NEW YORK TO RIO DE JANEIRO, BRAZIL

Air Facility
Courier Travel Service
Discount Travel International
Now Voyager

NEW YORK TO ROME, ITALY

Courier Travel Service
Discount Travel International
Halbart Express
Now Voyager

NEW YORK TO SAN JUAN, PUERTO RICO

Rush Courier

NEW YORK TO SANTIAGO, CHILE

Air Facility
Courier Travel Service
Discount Travel International
Now Voyager

NEW YORK TO SINGAPORE

Now Voyager

NEW YORK TO STOCKHOLM, SWEDEN

Courier Travel Service
Discount Travel International
Halbart Express
Now Voyager

NEW YORK TO TEL AVIV, ISRAEL

Courier Network
Courier Travel Service

NEW YORK TO TOKYO, JAPAN

Now Voyager
Polo Express

NEW YORK TO ZURICH, SWITZERLAND

Courier Travel Service
Discount Travel International
Halbart Express
Now Voyager

DESTINATIONS AVAILABLE FROM MIAMI, FLORIDA

MIAMI TO ASUNCION, PARAGUAY

Intertrade Courier International

MIAMI TO BOGOTA, COLUMBIA

Intertrade Courier International
LAC Express

MIAMI TO BUENOS AIRES, ARGENTINA

Intertrade Courier International
Line Haul Services

MIAMI TO CARACAS, VENEZUELA

A-1 International
Intertrade Courier International
Line Haul Services

MIAMI TO GUATEMALA CITY, GUATEMALA

Line Haul Services
Trans-Air System

MIAMI TO GUAYAQUIL, ECUADOR

Intertrade Courier International
Line Haul Services

MIAMI TO LA PAZ, BOLIVIA

Intertrade Courier International

MIAMI TO LIMA, PERU

Intertrade Courier International
Line Haul Services

MIAMI TO MADRID, SPAIN

Halbart Express

MIAMI TO MEXICO CITY, MEXICO

Intertrade Courier International

MIAMI TO MONTEVIDEO, URUGUAY

Intertrade Courier International

MIAMI TO PANAMA CITY, PANAMA

Intertrade Courier International
Line Haul Services

MIAMI TO QUITO, ECUADOR

Intertrade Courier International
Line Haul Services

MIAMI TO RIO DE JANEIRO, BRAZIL

Intertrade Courier International
Line Haul Services

MIAMI TO SAN JOSE, COSTA RICA

Line Haul Services
Trans-Air System

MIAMI TO SANTIAGO, CHILE

Intertrade Courier International
Line Haul Services

MIAMI TO SANTO DOMINGO, DOMINICAN REPUBLIC

Line Haul Services

DESTINATIONS AVAILABLE FROM LOS ANGELES, CALIFORNIA

LOS ANGELES TO BANGKOK, THAILAND

IBC Pacific, Inc.
Polo Express

LOS ANGELES TO DJAKARTA, INDONESIA

Way to Go Travel

LOS ANGELES TO HONG KONG

IBC Pacific, Inc.
Jupiter Air (Micom America)
Polo Express
Way to Go Travel

LOS ANGELES TO KUALA LUMPUR, MALAYSIA

Way to Go Travel

LOS ANGELES TO LONDON, ENGLAND

Midnite Express International Couriers
Polo Express

LOS ANGELES TO MELBOURNE, AUSTRALIA

Polo Express
Way to Go Travel

LOS ANGELES TO MEXICO CITY, MEXICO

SOS International Courier

LOS ANGELES TO PENANG, MALAYSIA

Way to Go Travel

LOS ANGELES TO SEOUL, KOREA

World Travel and Tours

LOS ANGELES TO SINGAPORE

IBC Pacific, Inc.
Jupiter Air (Micom America)
Way to Go Travel

LOS ANGELES TO SYDNEY, AUSTRALIA

Way to Go Travel

LOS ANGELES TO TOKYO, JAPAN

IBC Pacific, Inc.

DESTINATIONS AVAILABLE FROM SAN FRANCISCO, CALIFORNIA

SAN FRANCISCO TO BANGKOK, THAILAND

UTL Travel

SAN FRANCISCO TO HONG KONG

Jupiter Air, Ltd. (Micom America, Inc.)
Polo Express
UTL Travel
Way to Go Travel

SAN FRANCISCO TO LONDON, ENGLAND

Polo Express
UTL Travel

SAN FRANCISCO TO MANILA, PHILIPPINES

Jupiter Air, Ltd. (Micom America, Inc.)
UTL Travel

SAN FRANCISCO TO SINGAPORE

Jupiter Air, Ltd. (Micom America, Inc.)
Polo Express
UTL Travel
Way to Go Travel

DESTINATIONS AVAILABLE FROM HOUSTON, TEXAS

HOUSTON TO LONDON, ENGLAND

Now Voyager

HOUSTON TO TOKYO, JAPAN

Now Voyager

DESTINATIONS AVAILABLE FROM CHICAGO, ILLINOIS

CHICAGO TO MEXICO CITY, MEXICO

Leisure Marketing Corporation

ADDRESSES AND TELEPHONE NUMBERS OF ALL THE AIR COURIER COMPANIES REFERENCED ON THE PRECEDING PAGES

NEW YORK

Able Travel and Tours
18 East 41st Street
New York, NY 10017
(212) 779-8530

Air Facility
153-40 Rockaway Boulevard
Jamaica, NY 11434
(718) 712-0630
Fax: (718) 712-1574

Courier Network
295 7th Avenue
New York, NY 10001
(212) 691-9860
Fax: (212) 929-5186

Courier Travel Service
530 Central Avenue
Cedarhurst, NY 11516
(516) 374-2299
(800) 922-2FLY
(800) ASK-2FLY
Fax: (516) 374-2261

Discount Travel International (DTI)
152 West 72nd Street
New York, NY 10023
(212) 362-8113
Fax: (212) 362-5310

East-West Express
P.O. Box 30849
JFK Station
Jamaica, NY 11430
(516) 561-2360
Fax: (516) 568-0477

Halbart Express
147-05 176th Street
Jamaica, NY 11434
(718) 656-8189
Fax: (718) 244-0559

Intermail Courier
91-06 23rd Avenue
East Elmhurst, NY 11369
(718) 898-2526

Jupiter Air, Ltd. (Micom America, Inc.)
160-23 Rockaway Boulevard
Jamaica, NY 11434
(718) 341-2095
Fax: (718) 527-3763

Now Voyager
74 Varick Street
Suite 307
New York, NY 10013
(212) 431-1616
Fax: (212) 334-5243

Polo Express
160-23 Rockaway Boulevard
Jamaica, NY 11434
(718) 527 5546

Priority Air Freight NY, Ltd.
130-29 135th Avenue
South Ozone Park, NY 11420
(718) 529-1600
Fax: (718) 529-1657

Rush Courier
481 49th Street
Brooklyn, NY 11220
(718) 439-9043

World Courier, Inc.
137-42 Guy R. Brewer Boulevard
Jamaica, NY 11434
(800) 221-6600
Message Line Recording: (718) 978-9408
(718) 978-9552
Fax: (718) 276-6932

MIAMI

Halbart Express
2471 NW 72nd Avenue
Miami, FL 33122
(305) 593-0260
Fax: (305) 593-0158

Intertrade Courier International
7370 NW 36th Street
Suite 128
Miami, FL 33166
(305) 592-1700
Fax: (305) 592-7952

LAC Express
Box 523874
Miami, FL 33152
(305) 871-4737
Fax: (305) 876-0027

Line Haul Services
7859 NW 15th Street
Miami, FL 33126
(305) 477-0651
Fax: (305) 599-2002

Trans-Air System
7264 NW 25th Street
Miami, FL 33122
(305) 592-1771
Fax: (305) 592-2927

LOS ANGELES

IBC-Pacific
1595 East El Segundo Boulevard
El Segundo, CA 90245
(310) 607-0125
Fax: (310) 607-0126

Jupiter Air (Micom America)
6041 West Imperial Highway
Building 4, Section E
Los Angeles, CA 90045
(310) 670-5123
Fax: (310) 649-2771

Midnite Express International Couriers
930 West Hyde Park Boulevard
Inglewood, CA 90302
(310) 672-1100
Fax: (310) 671-0107

Polo Express
6011 Avion Drive
Suite 204
Los Angeles, CA 90045
(310) 410-6822
Fax: (310) 641-2966

SOS International Courier
8715 La Tijera Boulevard
Los Angeles, CA 90045
(310) 649-6640
Fax: (310) 649-1214

Way to Go Travel
6679 Sunset Boulevard
Hollywood, CA 90028
(213) 466-1126
Fax: (213) 466-8994

World Travel and Tours
3700 Wilshire Boulevard
Suite 200
Los Angeles, CA 90010
(213) 384-1000

SAN FRANCISCO

Jupiter Air, Ltd. (Micom America, Inc.)
Jal Cargo Terminal
North Access Road
San Francisco, CA 94128
(415) 872-6506
Fax: (415) 871-4975

Polo Express
238 Lawrence Avenue
Suite D
South San Francisco, CA 94080
(415) 742-9613
Fax: (415) 742-9614

UTL Travel
320 Corey Way
South San Francisco, CA 94080
(415) 583-5074
Fax: (415) 583-8122

Way to Go Travel
1850 Union Street
Suite 6
San Francisco, CA 94123
(415) 292-7801

HOUSTON

Now Voyager
(Has New York address and telephone numbers)
74 Varick Street
Suite 307
New York, NY 10013
(212) 431-1616
Fax: (212) 334-5243

CHICAGO

Leisure Marketing Corporation
2725 North Thatcher Avenue
Suite 210
River Grove, IL 60171
(708) 453-7300

SECTION
FOUR

FLYING ROUND-TRIP FROM A NON-U.S. GATEWAY CITY

London, England presently leads all other cities of the world in terms of numbers of destinations served. While New York currently boasts 24, London now tops the list with 36. However, New York has 14 courier companies compared to London's 3. Other Non-U.S. gateway countries include Canada; with Montreal having 2, Toronto 2, and Vancouver B.C. having 1. One note worth considering here about London departures: You can basically assume most flights are based out of Heathrow Airport, but it is very important you verify that Gatwick or some other large airport is not the designated point of departure/return.

The destinations available from England and Canada tend to be in a regular state of change, even more so than destinations served from U.S. gateways. Be sure to thoroughly explore all the options of all the courier companies (present and projected) before making up your mind.

Topping the list of requirements for a successful Non-U.S. gateway journey is the important concept of reliability and professionalism as discussed earlier. This concept grows even more important when you are dealing with Non-U.S. courier companies. The formality and etiquette typically displayed in countries such as England and Canada are typically carried over into the professional business environment which you will be dealing with. The bottom line is you will be doing yourself and the courier company the greatest service by being unquestionably reliable and professional. Keep in mind that the courier company will feel more confident of your availability, and you will be afforded with more flight chances and special opportunities.

As far as age and other operational requirements are concerned, the youngest you can typically be is 18, with maximum limits varying or non-existent. Methods of payment vary from personal check to credit cards, with options in-between possible. There is also a chance you can have your Frequent Flier account credited. Some companies require you to pre-register with them, while others do not have any such requirement. In any event, you can assume that the closer you are to the departure date, the lesser the fare you will be required to pay, and don't forget to negotiate!

The booking techniques detailed on pages 59 and 60 are very applicable, but keep in mind you will want to compare the fares of the various courier companies to make sure you are paying the lowest possible cost. Typically, these Non-U.S. fares vary even more so than the ones based out of the United States. Therefore, before you book, it will be to your benefit to explore all combinations and options. To further illustrate this, consider the fact that you might make unnecessary compromises with your plans in order to secure what seems to be a low fare, when just 'one other' courier company inquiry might have yielded you an even lower fare, with more certainty, flexibility, and less restrictions.

The last thing to actively consider are the baggage allowance rules of the various air courier companies. Like departures originating in the United States, these Non-U.S. courier companies

112

may allow you everything from two pieces of checked luggage to only one small carry-on bag. Be sure that you thoroughly understand all the options available to you, and that you weigh these options along with the cost of your ticket. Keep in mind that a slightly higher fare might be well worth it if you are allowed to check-in two large suitcases.

INTERNATIONAL DESTINATIONS AVAILABLE FROM LONDON, ENGLAND

LONDON TO ABU DHABI, UNITED ARAB EMIRATES

Polo Express
Shades Int.

LONDON TO AMSTERDAM, NETHERLANDS

Polo Express
Shades Int.

LONDON TO ATHENS, GREECE

Polo Express
Shades Int.

LONDON TO BANGKOK, THAILAND

Polo Express
Shades Int.

LONDON TO BARCELONA, SPAIN

Polo Express
Shades Int.

LONDON TO BERLIN, GERMANY

Polo Express
Shades Int.

LONDON TO BOSTON, MA U.S.A.

Polo Express
Shades Int.

LONDON TO CHICAGO, IL U.S.A.

Polo Express
Shades Int.

LONDON TO DALLAS, TX U.S.A.

Courier Travel Service

LONDON TO DETROIT, MI U.S.A.

Polo Express
Shades Int.

LONDON TO DUBAI, UNITED ARAB EMIRATES

Courier Travel Service
Polo Express
Shades Int.

LONDON TO GABORONE, BOTSWANA

Polo Express
Shades Int.

LONDON TO HONG KONG

Courier Travel Service
Polo Express
Shades Int.

LONDON TO JERSEY, ENGLAND

Polo Express
Shades Int.

LONDON TO JOHANNESBURG, SOUTH AFRICA

Courier Travel Service
Polo Express
Shades Int.

LONDON TO KUALA LUMPUR, MALAYSIA

Polo Express
Shades Int.

LONDON TO LISBON, PORTUGAL

Polo Express
Shades Int.

LONDON TO LOS ANGELES, CA U.S.A.

Courier Travel Service
Polo Express
Shades Int.

LONDON TO MIAMI, FL U.S.A.

Courier Travel Service
Polo Express
Shades Int.

LONDON TO MONTREAL, CANADA

Polo Express
Shades Int.

LONDON TO MUNICH, GERMANY

Polo Express
Shades Int.

LONDON TO NAIROBI, KENYA

Courier Travel Service
Polo Express
Shades Int.

LONDON TO NEWARK, NJ U.S.A.

Polo Express
Shades Int.

LONDON TO NEW YORK, NY U.S.A.

Courier Travel Service
Polo Express
Shades Int.

LONDON TO PARIS, FRANCE

Courier Travel Service

LONDON TO PHILADELPHIA, PA U.S.A.

Polo Express
Shades Int.

LONDON TO PITTSBURGH, PA U.S.A.

Polo Express

LONDON TO RIO DE JANERO, BRAZIL

Courier Travel Service

LONDON TO SAN FRANCISCO, CA U.S.A.

Courier Travel Service

LONDON TO SEATTLE, WA U.S.A.

Polo Express
Shades Int.

LONDON TO SINGAPORE

Polo Express
Shades Int.

LONDON TO SYDNEY, AUSTRALIA

Courier Travel Service
Polo Express
Shades Int.

LONDON TO TEL AVIV, ISRAEL

Polo Express
Shades Int.

LONDON TO TOKYO, JAPAN

Courier Travel Service

LONDON TO TORONTO, CANADA

Courier Travel Service
Polo Express
Shades Int.

LONDON TO WASHINGTON, D.C. U.S.A.

Polo Express
Shades Int.

INTERNATIONAL DESTINATIONS AVAILABLE FROM MONTREAL, CANADA

MONTREAL TO LONDON, ENGLAND

F.B. On-Board Courier

MONTREAL TO PARIS, FRANCE

F.B. On-Board Courier
Jet Services

INTERNATIONAL DESTINATIONS AVAILABLE FROM TORONTO, CANADA

TORONTO TO HONG KONG

F.B. On-Board Courier

TORONTO TO LONDON, ENGLAND

F.B. On-Board Courier

INTERNATIONAL DESTINATIONS AVAILABLE FROM VANCOUVER B.C., CANADA

VANCOUVER TO LONDON, ENGLAND

F.B. On-Board Courier

ADDRESSES AND TELEPHONE NUMBERS OF INTERNATIONAL AIR COURIER COMPANIES REFERENCED ON THE PRECEDING PAGES

LONDON

Courier Travel Services
346 Fulham Rd.
London, England SW109UH
071-351-0300 (U.S. dial: 011-44-71-351-0300)
Fax: 071-351-0170 (U.S. dial: 011-44-71-351-0170)

Polo
208 Epsom Square
London Heathrow Airport, Hounslow
Middlesex, England TW6 2BL
081-759-5383 (U.S. dial: 011-44-81-759-5383)
Fax: 081-759-5697 (U.S. dial: 011-44-81-759-5697)

MONTREAL

F.B. On-Board Courier Services
10105 Ryan Ave.
Dorval, Quebec H9P1A2
514-633-0951

Jet Services
2735 Paulus St.
Ville St. Laurent
Montreal, Quebec H4S 1E9
514-331-7470
Fax: 514-331-3451
1-800-361-4969 (In Canada Only)

TORONTO

F.B. On-Board Courier Services
10105 Ryan Ave.
Dorval, Quebec H9P1A2
514-633-0951

VANCOUVER, B.C.

F.B. On-Board Courier Services
5200 Miller Rd., Suite #116
Richmond, British Columbia V7B 1X8
604-278-1266

SECTION
FIVE

SUMMARY

If you followed through with all the directions and suggestions in this book, you should now have a very complete theoretical and practical knowledge of the air courier business.

The industry is constantly changing. Destinations come and go, along with some of the air courier companies themselves.

Some of the best situations occur when a prospective traveler is pleasantly surprised with the availability of a destination and time that coincides with some hopeful plans. Unexpected and pleasant experiences can also happen when the destination and time are a total surprise at the last minute to the hopeful traveler.

Whatever your motivation for air courier travel, whether you are a business person/entrepreneur, a teacher, retiree, a wise shopper, or simply an adventurous person that wants to see the world, we hope this book has assisted you in getting started.

We wish you the best and safest journey possible, and hope that air courier travel will open up many new doors in your life.

FREQUENTLY ASKED QUESTIONS

Q: When an air courier company introduces a
      new destination, will an extra special fare be
      temporarily available?

A: Generally yes. When inquiring about new
      routes, be sure to ask the air courier
      company if a special introductory fare will be
      offered. Also, be sure to ask them how much
      this special fare is, and how long it will be in
      effect.

Q: Is it possible to fly aboard the Concorde as a
      courier?

A: Yes it's possible. For the most likely
      opportunity, contact air courier companies
      which service the New York to London route.

Q: Do air couriers need any special training?

A: No, not any formal training. An individual
      will be well suited for courier travel after
      studying this book.

Q: Does the airfare quoted to me by the air courier company include any applicable departure taxes?

A: No. You can count on paying this amount separately as required. Depending on the airport involved, you could pay as little as a few dollars, or upwards of forty dollars.

Q: Presently, what is the most heavily traveled courier route?

A: New York to London.

Q: Do air couriers usually travel on the major airlines?

A: Air couriers always travel on the major airlines, and they blend right in with all the other passengers. No special provisions are made for air courier travelers.

Q: What happens if an air courier's flight is canceled by the airlines?

A: The courier is usually placed aboard the next flight out.